I0490572

Pivot or Perish: The Entrepreneur's Guide to Navigating Turbulent Times and Coming Out on Top

SaPH

Pivot or Perish: The Entrepreneur's Guide to Navigating Turbulent Times
and Coming Out on Top

ISBN-13: 979-8-3920-8106-6

Pivot or Perish: The Entrepreneur's Guide to Navigating Turbulent Times and Coming Out on Top

CONTENTS

Pivot or Perish: The Entrepreneur's Guide to Navigating Turbulent Times and Coming Out on Top

Are you an entrepreneur who's feeling overwhelmed by the fast-paced and constantly-changing business landscape? Are you struggling to keep up with the latest trends and stay ahead of the competition? If so, "Pivot or Perish" is the book you've been waiting for.

In this groundbreaking guide, you'll discover the secrets of successful entrepreneurs who have mastered the art of pivoting - adapting and evolving in response to changing market conditions. You'll learn how to identify disruptive forces, anticipate market shifts, and make the right strategic pivots that will enable you to thrive in any environment.

Unlike other business books that offer vague platitudes and generic advice, "Pivot or Perish" provides a step-by-step roadmap for navigating the twists and turns of entrepreneurship. You'll learn how to assess your strengths and weaknesses, identify untapped opportunities, and develop innovative products and services that meet the evolving needs of your customers.

Whether you're a startup founder or a seasoned business owner, "Pivot or Perish" will give you the tools and strategies you need to stay ahead of the curve and achieve long-term success. With its compelling real-world examples, actionable insights, and expert advice, this book is a must-read for anyone who wants to build a business that can withstand any challenge and come out on top. Don't wait - pick up your copy today and start pivoting towards success!

Chapter 1: The Case for Pivoting

Pivoting is essential in today's business environment for several reasons. Firstly, the speed of change in markets and industries has accelerated dramatically in recent years, driven in part by the rise of digital technologies and the global economy. This means that businesses that fail to pivot and adapt to changing market conditions risk falling behind their competitors and losing market share.

Secondly, disruptive technologies and business models are constantly emerging, challenging traditional industries and creating new opportunities. By pivoting, businesses can take advantage of these trends and position themselves for success in the future.

Thirdly, customer expectations and preferences are evolving rapidly, with consumers increasingly demanding personalized, tailored experiences from the businesses they interact with. By pivoting, businesses can stay responsive to changing customer needs and preferences and maintain a customer-centric approach.

Finally, pivoting can help businesses to stay agile and nimble in the face of uncertainty and volatility. By being willing to change direction as needed, businesses can respond quickly to unexpected events and mitigate risks.

One of the biggest misconceptions about pivoting is that it's a sign of failure. Many entrepreneurs and business owners are hesitant to pivot because they believe that changing direction is a sign that their initial idea or strategy was flawed. However, this couldn't be further from the truth. Pivoting is a natural and necessary part of the entrepreneurial journey, and successful entrepreneurs understand that it's better to pivot early and often than to stick with a failing strategy.

Another misconception about pivoting is that it's a radical and dramatic change. While pivoting can sometimes involve a significant shift in strategy or direction, it can also be a subtle and gradual process. It's not always about completely abandoning your original idea or business model - sometimes it's about making small tweaks and adjustments along the way to stay on track and adapt to changing circumstances.

Finally, some entrepreneurs and business owners may be hesitant to pivot because they are afraid of the unknown. It can be daunting to make a significant change and step into uncharted territory. However, successful pivots are often based on careful analysis, research, and testing, and involve a calculated risk rather than blind leap of faith.

By addressing these misconceptions and understanding the true nature of pivoting, readers will be better equipped to embrace the strategy and take advantage of the benefits it offers.

There are many examples of successful pivots that have had a significant impact on businesses and industries. Here are a few real-world examples:

> **PayPal:** Originally founded as a company that created software to encrypt data on handheld devices, PayPal pivoted to become a leading online payment platform. The company recognized the potential of the internet as a payment platform and pivoted to take advantage of this opportunity, ultimately becoming one of the most successful fintech companies in the world.

> **Instagram:** Originally launched as a check-in app called Burbn, Instagram pivoted to focus exclusively on photo-sharing. This pivot proved to be a wise decision, as the app quickly gained popularity and was eventually acquired by Facebook for $1 billion.

> **Netflix:** Originally founded as a DVD-by-mail rental service, Netflix pivoted to become a streaming video platform, recognizing the shift in consumer preferences towards on-demand content. This pivot has proven hugely successful, with Netflix becoming one of the world's most popular entertainment platforms.

> **Nokia:** Nokia was once a leading mobile phone manufacturer, but with the rise of smartphones, the company struggled to keep up with competitors like Apple

and Samsung. In a bold pivot, Nokia sold its phone business to Microsoft and refocused its efforts on building network infrastructure for telecommunications providers. This pivot has allowed Nokia to stay relevant in a rapidly changing industry.

➢ **Groupon:** Originally launched as a platform for collective buying deals, Groupon pivoted to become a local e-commerce marketplace. This pivot allowed Groupon to diversify its offerings and provide a wider range of services to its customers, ultimately leading to greater success.

In each of these cases, the pivot allowed the company to take advantage of new opportunities, respond to changing market conditions, and ultimately achieve greater success than they would have if they had stuck with their original business models.

Chapter 2: Assessing Your Business

Evaluating the strengths and weaknesses of your business is an important step in determining whether or not a pivot is necessary. Here are some steps you can take to evaluate your business:

Conducting a SWOT analysis can provide a comprehensive view of your business's current situation, and help you identify key areas for improvement and growth.

In a SWOT analysis, you'll typically identify:

Strengths are the internal factors that your business excels at, and they can be a powerful advantage in the market. Here are some examples of strengths that a business might have:

> **Unique product or service offerings:** A business may have a product or service that is differentiated from competitors in some way, such as superior quality, better features, or more affordable pricing.

> **Strong brand recognition:** A business with a well-established brand can benefit from customer loyalty, increased visibility, and a competitive advantage in the market.

> **Talented team:** A business with a team of skilled and motivated employees can drive innovation, deliver high-quality products and services, and create a positive work culture.

> **Efficient operations:** A business that operates efficiently and effectively can reduce costs, increase productivity, and improve customer satisfaction.

> **Strong financial position:** A business with strong financials, such as a healthy cash flow, high profitability, or low debt, can have more flexibility in pursuing growth opportunities and weathering economic downturns.

Weaknesses are the internal factors that your business struggles with, and they can hinder your ability to compete in the market. Here are some examples of weaknesses that a business might have:

> **Lack of resources or expertise:** A business may struggle to compete due to a lack of resources, such as capital, technology, or skilled employees. This can hinder the business's ability to innovate, expand, or deliver high-quality products and services.

> **Poor financial performance:** A business with low profitability, high debt, or cash flow issues may struggle to invest in growth opportunities or weather economic downturns.

> **Outdated technology:** A business with outdated technology may struggle to keep up with competitors and may be less efficient or effective in delivering products and services.

> **Ineffective marketing or branding:** A business with weak branding or marketing may struggle to attract and retain customers, and may not effectively communicate its value proposition.

> **Poor customer service:** A business that delivers poor customer service may struggle to retain customers and may damage its reputation.

Opportunities are the external factors that could benefit your business, and they can create new possibilities for growth and success. Here are some examples of opportunities that a business might have:

> **Growing market:** A business may be operating in a market that is expanding or experiencing strong demand, creating opportunities for growth and expansion.

> **Emerging trends:** A business may be well-positioned to capitalize on emerging trends in its industry, such as new

technologies, changing consumer preferences, or regulatory changes.

➢ **Strategic partnerships:** A business may have opportunities to form strategic partnerships or collaborations with other businesses or organizations, which can provide access to new markets, customers, or resources.

➢ **International expansion:** A business may have opportunities to expand its operations into new geographic markets, tapping into new customer bases and revenue streams.

➢ **Changes in the competitive landscape:** A business may have opportunities to gain market share or differentiate itself from competitors due to changes in the competitive landscape, such as the exit of a major competitor or the introduction of a new product or service.

Threats are the external factors that could harm your business, and they can pose significant risks to your operations and financial performance. Here are some examples of threats that a business might face:

➢ **New competitors:** A business may face increased competition from new market entrants, which can erode market share and pricing power.

➢ **Economic downturns:** A business may be vulnerable to economic downturns or recessionary periods, which can lead to reduced demand for its products or services and lower revenue.

➢ **Changes in regulations:** A business may face regulatory changes or compliance requirements, which can increase costs and limit business operations.

➢ **Technological disruption:** A business may face

disruption from new technologies or changing industry trends, which can render existing products or services obsolete.

➢ **Natural disasters or other external events:** A business may face external events such as natural disasters, political instability, or public health crises that can disrupt operations, supply chains, and customer demand.

Once you've identified your business's strengths, weaknesses, opportunities, and threats, you can use this information to develop strategies to address each area. For example, you may decide to invest in new technology to address a weakness, or develop a marketing campaign to capitalize on an opportunity.

Overall, conducting a SWOT analysis can help you take a step back and evaluate your business objectively, so you can make informed decisions and take actions that will improve your chances of success.

Reviewing your financial statements is an important part of evaluating the strengths and weaknesses of your business. Financial statements such as your balance sheet and income statement provide valuable insights into your business's financial health and performance. Here's how you can use financial statements to identify areas where your business is performing well and where it may be struggling:

➢ **Balance sheet:** Your balance sheet provides a snapshot of your business's financial position at a given point in time. By reviewing your balance sheet, you can assess your business's liquidity, leverage, and asset and liability management. For example, you can identify if you have a healthy cash position, if you have too much debt, or if you have assets that are not generating a sufficient return.

➢ **Income statement:** Your income statement shows your

business's revenue and expenses over a specific period of time. By reviewing your income statement, you can assess your business's profitability and operational efficiency. For example, you can identify if your revenue is growing, if your expenses are under control, or if you are generating a healthy profit margin.

Conducting market research is an important step in evaluating your business's strengths and weaknesses. By conducting market research, you can gather information about your target audience, their needs and preferences, and the competitive landscape in which your business operates. Here's how you can use market research to identify areas where your business may be falling behind and where you may need to improve:

Customer feedback is an important component of market research that can help you identify areas where your business may need to improve. Here are some ways you can gather customer feedback:

➢ **Surveys:** You can use online surveys to gather feedback from your customers. Surveys can be designed to ask specific questions about your products or services, customer experience, and overall satisfaction. You can distribute surveys via email, social media, or on your website.

➢ **Focus groups:** Focus groups are a more interactive way to gather feedback from your customers. You can invite a small group of customers to participate in a group discussion or activity where they can share their thoughts and opinions about your products or services.

➢ **Interviews:** One-on-one interviews with customers can provide in-depth insights into their experiences and preferences. You can conduct interviews in person, over the phone, or via video conferencing.

When gathering customer feedback, it's important to ask open-ended questions and to listen carefully to their responses. You should also be prepared to act on the feedback you receive by making changes to your products or services based on the feedback you receive. By listening to your customers, you can identify areas where your business may need to improve and make changes to meet their needs and preferences.

Conducting a competitor analysis is an important part of market research that can help you understand the competitive landscape and identify areas where your business may need to improve. Here are some steps you can take to conduct a competitor analysis:

> **Identify your competitors:** Make a list of your main competitors in your industry or market.

> **Research their products or services:** Look at the features, quality, and pricing of your competitors' products or services. Identify areas where your products or services may be falling behind.

> **Analyze their marketing strategies:** Look at how your competitors are promoting their products or services. Are they using social media, email marketing, or other forms of advertising? Identify areas where your marketing strategies may need to improve.

> **Analyze their pricing strategies:** Look at how your competitors are pricing their products or services. Are they offering discounts or other promotions? Identify areas where your pricing strategies may need to improve.

> **Identify their strengths and weaknesses:** Based on your research, identify your competitors' strengths and weaknesses. Use this information to identify opportunities for your business to differentiate itself from its competitors.

Staying up-to-date on industry trends is an important part of conducting market research and can help you identify new opportunities and areas where you may need to adapt. Here are some steps you can take to stay informed about industry trends:

➢ **Research industry publications:** Subscribe to industry publications, such as trade magazines or newsletters, to stay informed about new developments and trends in your industry.

➢ **Attend industry events:** Attend industry events, such as conferences or trade shows, to learn about new technologies, products, or services and network with other professionals in your industry.

➢ **Network with other professionals:** Connect with other professionals in your industry through networking events, social media, or professional organizations to stay informed about new trends and developments.

➢ **Follow industry influencers:** Follow thought leaders and influencers in your industry on social media or through their blogs to stay informed about new trends and developments.

Seeking feedback from customers and employees is an important step in identifying areas where your business is succeeding and where it may need improvement. Here are some ways to gather feedback:

➢ **Surveys:** Surveys can be a great way to gather feedback from customers and employees. You can create online surveys using tools like SurveyMonkey or Google Forms and distribute them via email or social media.

➢ **Focus groups:** Focus groups are a small group of customers or employees who are brought together to provide feedback on a specific product or service. This can be a great way to get more in-depth feedback and insights.

➢ **Interviews:** You can also conduct one-on-one interviews with customers or employees to gather more detailed feedback.

> **Social media:** Social media can be a great way to gather feedback from customers. You can create polls on Facebook or Twitter, or ask for feedback in the comments section of your posts.

Evaluating your team is an important part of understanding your business's potential for success. This includes both your own strengths and weaknesses as a leader, as well as the strengths and weaknesses of your team members. By identifying areas where your team may be lacking, you can determine whether it is necessary to hire new talent or invest in additional training.

Start by assessing your own leadership style and strengths. Are you a strong communicator? Do you have a clear vision for the business? Are you effective at delegating tasks? Identifying areas where you excel as a leader can help you leverage those strengths to benefit your team and business.

Next, evaluate each team member's skills and performance. Consider whether they have the necessary expertise and experience to excel in their roles. Are they meeting their goals and contributing to the overall success of the business? Are there any areas where they may need additional training or support?

It may also be helpful to consider how your team works together. Are there any communication or collaboration issues that need to be addressed? Are there any personality conflicts that may be affecting productivity? By identifying these issues, you can take steps to improve team dynamics and create a more cohesive and productive work environment.

Finally, consider whether there are any gaps in your team's skills or expertise that need to be filled. This may involve hiring new talent or investing in additional training for your current team. By doing so, you can ensure that your team has the necessary skills and expertise to navigate any challenges that may arise in the future.

By taking these steps to evaluate your business, you can gain a better understanding of your strengths and weaknesses, as well as the opportunities and challenges facing your business. This can help you make informed decisions about whether or not a pivot is necessary and what direction your business should take moving forward.

Techniques for identifying untapped opportunities and potential threats

Here are some techniques for identifying untapped opportunities and potential threats:

SWOT analysis is an effective technique for identifying untapped opportunities and potential threats. As mentioned earlier, SWOT stands for Strengths, Weaknesses, Opportunities, and Threats. By conducting a SWOT analysis, you can gain a better understanding of your business's internal strengths and weaknesses, as well as external opportunities and threats.

To conduct a SWOT analysis, you can start by gathering a team of stakeholders from your business, including managers, employees, and even customers. Then, you can brainstorm and identify the internal and external factors that affect your business.

For strengths and weaknesses, you can look at internal factors such as your company's culture, resources, processes, products, and services. For opportunities and threats, you can look at external factors such as market trends, competition, regulations, and technological advancements.

Once you have identified these factors, you can create a matrix with four quadrants: Strengths, Weaknesses, Opportunities, and Threats. Then, you can plot each factor in the appropriate quadrant. This will help you visualize the areas where your business is performing well and where it needs improvement, as well as the areas where you can take advantage of opportunities or mitigate threats.

By conducting a SWOT analysis, you can identify untapped

opportunities and potential threats that may not have been immediately obvious. This can help you make more informed decisions and develop strategies to pivot your business and stay competitive in a changing market.

A PEST analysis can help you identify macro-environmental factors that may impact your business. Here's a brief overview of each factor:

> **Political:** Political factors include government policies and regulations that may impact your business, such as taxes, trade policies, and labor laws.

> **Economic:** Economic factors include trends in the economy that may impact your business, such as inflation, interest rates, and consumer spending.

> **Social:** Social factors include demographic trends and cultural influences that may impact your business, such as changing consumer preferences or attitudes towards certain products.

> **Technological:** Technological factors include advancements in technology that may impact your business, such as new software or hardware, automation, or changes in communication channels.

Conducting customer surveys can help you identify unmet needs and areas for improvement in your products or services. You can use surveys to gather feedback on your customers' satisfaction with your products or services, their overall experience with your business, and their preferences and needs. This can help you identify areas where you may need to make improvements or changes to better meet the needs of your customers. Surveys can be conducted through online tools, email, or phone calls, and should be designed to be concise, focused, and easy to understand.

Analyzing your competitors is a crucial part of any business strategy. By understanding what your competitors are offering, how they are marketing their products or services, and how much they are charging for them, you can identify areas where you may need to improve in order to remain competitive.

When conducting a competitor analysis, there are several key areas to consider:

> **Products or services:** Start by analyzing your competitors' products or services. Look at their features, quality, and pricing. Are they offering something that you are not? Are their products or services priced higher or lower than yours?

> **Marketing strategies:** Look at how your competitors are promoting their products or services. Consider their advertising channels, messaging, and branding. Are they targeting a different audience than you? Are they using social media or other digital marketing channels that you are not?

> **Pricing strategies:** Evaluate your competitors' pricing strategies. Consider their pricing structure, discounts, and promotions. Are they pricing their products or services higher or lower than yours? Are they offering any special deals or packages that you are not?

> **Strengths and weaknesses:** Finally, consider your competitors' strengths and weaknesses. Look at their online reviews, ratings, and customer feedback to identify areas where they excel and areas where they may be falling short. This can help you identify areas where you may need to improve in order to stay competitive.

Industry research can help you identify emerging trends, changing consumer preferences, and new technologies that may impact your business. This information can be gathered through a variety of sources such as industry publications, market research reports, and attending industry events or conferences. By staying informed about industry trends, you can position your business to take advantage of new opportunities and stay ahead of potential threats.

Some ways to conduct industry research include:

> **Industry publications:** Subscribe to industry-specific publications such as trade magazines, newsletters, or blogs. These publications often provide in-depth coverage of industry trends, news, and developments.

> **Market research reports:** Purchase market research reports from reputable research firms that focus on your industry. These reports often provide valuable insights into market trends, consumer behavior, and competitive analysis.

> **Industry events:** Attend industry events such as conferences, trade shows, or networking events. These events provide opportunities to learn about new technologies, products, and services in your industry and to network with other professionals in your field.

> **Online resources:** Use online resources such as social media, forums, or online communities to stay informed about industry news and developments. LinkedIn groups or industry-specific subreddits can be great sources of information and networking opportunities.

Gathering feedback from your employees is a valuable technique for identifying untapped opportunities and potential threats in your business. Your employees are on the front lines of your operations and can provide valuable insights into areas where your business may be falling short.

One way to gather employee feedback is through regular check-ins and performance reviews. These meetings provide an opportunity to discuss the employee's performance and any areas where they may need additional support or training. You can also use these meetings to gather feedback on your operations and identify areas where you may need to make improvements.

Another way to gather employee feedback is through surveys or focus groups. These can be conducted anonymously to encourage honest feedback. You can ask questions about employee satisfaction, company culture, and areas for improvement. This feedback can help you identify areas where you may need to make changes to improve employee morale and productivity.

By gathering feedback from your employees, you can identify areas for improvement in your operations, culture, or team dynamics. This can help you address any potential threats to your business and identify untapped opportunities for growth. Additionally, by involving your employees in the decision-making process, you can improve employee morale and foster a culture of collaboration and innovation.

Innovation workshops or brainstorming sessions are great techniques for identifying untapped opportunities. These sessions involve bringing together a diverse group of people from different departments or teams within your organization to generate new ideas and explore potential opportunities.

During these sessions, encourage your team to think outside the box and come up with creative solutions to problems or challenges. You can use different ideation techniques such as mind mapping, reverse thinking, or SWOT analysis to facilitate the process.

It's important to create a safe and non-judgmental environment that encourages open communication and collaboration. Encourage everyone to participate and share their ideas, regardless of their role or level within the organization.

Once you've generated a list of potential ideas or opportunities, evaluate them based on their feasibility and potential impact on your business. This can help you prioritize which ideas to pursue and invest resources in.

Innovation workshops can help your organization stay ahead of the curve and identify new opportunities that can lead to growth and success.

Developing a roadmap for strategic pivots involves a series of steps to ensure that the pivot is planned and executed effectively. Here are some key steps to consider when developing a roadmap for strategic pivots:

Define the objective: The first step in developing a roadmap for strategic pivots is to clearly define the objective. What is the goal of the pivot? Is it to enter a new market, introduce a new product, or change the business model? Having a clear objective will help guide the rest of the planning process.

Defining the objective is crucial when developing a roadmap for strategic pivots. It helps ensure that everyone is aligned on the intended outcome and provides a clear direction for decision-making. Without a clear objective, it can be challenging to develop a roadmap that is effective in achieving the desired outcome. The objective should be specific, measurable, achievable, relevant, and time-bound (SMART) to ensure that it is actionable and can be tracked for progress. Once the objective is defined, the next step is to assess the current state of the business and identify any gaps or opportunities for improvement.

Conduct research: Once the objective is defined, conduct research to identify potential opportunities and challenges. This may involve market research, competitor analysis, and internal analysis to identify strengths, weaknesses, opportunities, and threats (SWOT analysis).

Develop a plan: Based on the research conducted, develop a plan that outlines the steps required to achieve the objective. This should include timelines, milestones, and key performance indicators (KPIs) to track progress.

Developing a plan is a crucial step in developing a roadmap for strategic pivots. This plan should be based on the research conducted and should clearly outline the steps required to achieve the objective. The plan should include timelines, milestones, and KPIs to track progress. It should also consider potential challenges and risks and identify ways to mitigate them. Additionally, the plan should include a budget and resource allocation plan. The plan should be well-structured, realistic, and flexible to accommodate changes as the pivot progresses.

Communicate the plan: Communicate the plan to stakeholders, including employees, investors, and customers, to ensure everyone is aligned and understands the pivot.

Communicating the plan is an essential step in the process of strategic pivots. It is important to ensure that all stakeholders are on the same page and understand the reason for the pivot and the plan for achieving it. Communication can take various forms such as meetings, presentations, emails, or newsletters. It is also important to address any concerns or questions that stakeholders may have to build trust and confidence in the plan.

Implementing the plan will involve executing the specific steps outlined in the plan to achieve the defined objective. This may include making changes to the organization's structure, processes, or systems to align with the new strategy. It's important to monitor progress regularly and make adjustments as needed to ensure the pivot is successful.

Monitoring progress is an essential step in the roadmap for strategic pivots. It enables the team to evaluate whether the pivot is on track to achieve its objectives and to identify any areas that require adjustment. By monitoring progress, the team can also identify any unanticipated challenges that may arise during the pivot and develop solutions to overcome them. Additionally, it can help the team identify any unexpected benefits that may have resulted from the pivot. Overall, monitoring progress is critical to ensuring that the pivot is successful and achieves its intended outcomes.

Iterating and adjusting the plan is an important step in the process of developing a roadmap for strategic pivots. It is crucial to continuously monitor progress against the KPIs identified in the plan and adjust the plan as needed to ensure that the pivot is successful. This may involve making changes to the strategy, adjusting timelines, or reallocating resources to address any challenges or opportunities that arise during the implementation process. By being flexible and adaptable, a business can increase its chances of success when making strategic pivots.

Chapter 3: Anticipating Disruptive Forces

The key trends and technologies that are transforming industries
There are several key trends and technologies that are currently transforming industries. Here are a few:

> **Artificial Intelligence (AI):** AI has the potential to transform almost every industry by automating processes, improving efficiency, and enhancing decision-making. It is already being used in areas such as healthcare, finance, and customer service.

> **Internet of Things (IoT):** IoT refers to the connection of everyday objects to the internet. This technology is transforming industries such as transportation, manufacturing, and energy by enabling remote monitoring, predictive maintenance, and real-time data analytics.

> **Augmented Reality (AR) and Virtual Reality (VR):** AR and VR technologies are transforming industries such as gaming, education, and healthcare by providing immersive experiences and simulations.

> **Blockchain:** Blockchain technology has the potential to revolutionize industries such as finance and supply chain management by providing secure and transparent transactions.

> **Renewable Energy:** The shift towards renewable energy sources such as solar and wind power is transforming the energy industry and enabling greater sustainability.

> **Big Data:** The explosion of data is transforming industries such as healthcare, finance, and marketing by enabling more informed decision-making and personalized experiences for customers.

> **5G Technology:** The rollout of 5G technology is transforming industries such as telecommunications, healthcare, and transportation by enabling faster and more

reliable connectivity, as well as the development of new technologies such as autonomous vehicles.

How to stay ahead of the curve and anticipate market shifts?

Staying ahead of the curve and anticipating market shifts is essential for businesses to remain competitive and relevant. Here are some strategies for doing so:

> **Monitor industry trends:** Stay up-to-date on industry news, publications, and events to identify emerging trends and shifts in the market.

> **Engage with customers:** Regularly engage with your customers to understand their needs, preferences, and pain points. This will help you anticipate shifts in the market and adjust your strategy accordingly.

> **Monitor your competitors:** Keep a close eye on your competitors to understand their strengths and weaknesses, as well as their product and marketing strategies. This will help you identify potential threats and opportunities in the market.

> **Foster a culture of innovation:** Encourage innovation and experimentation within your organization to identify new products, services, or business models that can adapt to market shifts.

> **Leverage data analytics:** Utilize data analytics to track and analyze customer behavior, market trends, and industry shifts. This will help you identify patterns and make data-driven decisions.

> **Stay agile:** Be prepared to pivot quickly in response to market shifts. This may involve adjusting your strategy, reallocating resources, or introducing new products or services.

> ➤ **Develop strategic partnerships:** Partner with other businesses or organizations to leverage their expertise and stay ahead of the curve. This may involve collaborating on research and development, sharing industry insights, or pooling resources.

By employing these strategies, businesses can stay ahead of the curve and anticipate market shifts, giving them a competitive advantage and ensuring long-term success.

To stay ahead of the curve and anticipate market shifts, businesses need to be proactive in identifying warning signs of disruption and adapting to change. Here are some strategies to consider:

> ➤ **Conduct regular market research:** Keep a finger on the pulse of the market by conducting regular market research to identify new trends, technologies, and potential disruptors. This can include analyzing competitor activities, tracking customer behavior, and monitoring industry publications and news sources.

> ➤ **Stay connected with customers:** Engage with customers regularly through surveys, focus groups, and other feedback mechanisms to understand their needs and identify areas for improvement. This can help businesses anticipate market shifts and adapt to changing customer preferences.

> ➤ **Network with industry experts:** Attend industry conferences, join industry groups, and network with other professionals in your field to stay informed about new developments and emerging trends. This can also help businesses build relationships and partnerships that can be valuable in adapting to change.

> ➤ **Foster a culture of innovation:** Encourage innovation and creativity within your organization by providing

resources and support for experimentation, brainstorming, and idea generation. This can help businesses stay ahead of the curve and anticipate market shifts.

➢ **Invest in training and development:** Provide ongoing training and development opportunities for employees to keep their skills and knowledge up-to-date. This can help businesses stay agile and adapt to changes in the market.

➢ **Monitor key performance indicators:** Establish key performance indicators (KPIs) to track progress and identify warning signs of disruption. This can include metrics such as customer acquisition and retention rates, revenue growth, and market share.

➢ **Be open to change:** Finally, businesses need to be open to change and willing to pivot when necessary. This may involve making strategic shifts in the business model, product or service offerings, or marketing strategy. By being proactive and adaptable, businesses can stay ahead of the curve and succeed in a rapidly changing marketplace.

Chapter 4: Making the Right Pivots

Evaluating different pivot options and choosing the right strategy for your business can be a complex process. Here are some steps to help you evaluate your options and choose the best pivot strategy for your business:

Analyzing the current situation of your business is a crucial step in identifying potential pivot options and selecting the best strategy. This involves conducting an in-depth analysis of your business, as well as the market and industry in which you operate. Here are some key steps to follow when analyzing your current situation:

➢ **Conduct a SWOT analysis:** A SWOT analysis helps you identify the internal strengths and weaknesses of your business, as well as external opportunities and threats in the market. This analysis can help you identify areas where your business is excelling and where it needs improvement.

➢ **Analyze your financials:** Take a close look at your financial statements to identify any areas of concern, such as declining revenues or rising expenses. This analysis can help you identify any financial constraints or opportunities that may impact your pivot options.

➢ **Conduct market research:** Conducting market research can help you understand the competitive landscape, as well as identify emerging trends and shifts in customer behavior. This information can help you identify new market opportunities or threats that may impact your business.

➢ **Assess your team:** Your team plays a critical role in the success of your pivot strategy. Assessing the skills and capabilities of your team can help you identify areas where additional talent may be needed to support your pivot efforts.

➢ **Evaluate your current product/service offerings:** Assess your current product or service offerings to identify areas where you may need to make changes to better align with market demand. This can help you identify potential pivot options that may require changes to your existing offerings.

Once you have completed an analysis of your current situation, you can then use this information to evaluate potential pivot options and select the right strategy for your business. By understanding your strengths and weaknesses, as well as the market opportunities and threats, you can make informed decisions that will position your business for success in the long term.

Identifying potential pivot options is an important step in the process of choosing the right strategy for your business. Here are some strategies to consider when brainstorming pivot options:

➢ **Explore new markets:** One potential pivot option is to explore new markets. This could involve targeting new customer segments or expanding your business into new geographic regions. Conduct market research to identify areas of unmet customer needs or underserved markets.

➢ **Develop new products or services:** Another pivot option is to develop new products or services. Look for ways to innovate and differentiate your offerings from those of your competitors. Consider how emerging technologies or changing consumer preferences could be leveraged to create new products or services.

➢ **Change your business model:** A third pivot option is to change your business model. This could involve shifting from a product-based to a service-based business, or vice versa. It could also involve adopting a subscription-based model, or changing your pricing strategy.

➢ **Partner with other businesses:** Partnering with other businesses can also be a pivot option. Consider forming strategic partnerships or joint ventures with other companies to leverage their expertise, resources, or customer base.

➢ **Acquire other businesses:** Another pivot option is to acquire other businesses. This can help you enter new markets or gain access to new technologies or products. However, it is important to carefully evaluate the potential risks and benefits of any acquisition before proceeding.

➢ **Focus on new channels or distribution methods:** Consider exploring new channels or distribution methods to reach new customers. This could involve developing an e-commerce platform, partnering with third-party retailers, or leveraging social media and influencer marketing.

Conducting a feasibility analysis is a crucial step in evaluating potential pivot options for your business. This analysis helps you determine which options are realistic and achievable, based on factors such as cost, resources required, and potential return on investment. Here are some key steps to follow when conducting a feasibility analysis:

➢ **Define the criteria:** Start by defining the criteria for evaluating each potential pivot option. This may include factors such as the cost of implementation, the potential revenue or cost savings, the level of competition in the new market, and the availability of resources required to execute the pivot.

➢ **Gather information:** Gather information on each potential pivot option, including market research, competitive analysis, and financial projections. This information will help you evaluate the feasibility of each option against the criteria you have defined.

➢ **Evaluate the options:** Evaluate each potential pivot option against the criteria you have defined. Identify the strengths and weaknesses of each option, and assess the level of risk associated with each one.

> **Prioritize the options:** Once you have evaluated each potential pivot option, prioritize them based on their feasibility and potential impact on your business. Consider the level of investment required to execute each pivot option, as well as the potential return on investment.

> **Make a decision:** Based on your feasibility analysis and prioritization, make a decision on which pivot option to pursue. Consider factors such as the level of risk, the potential impact on your business, and the resources required to execute the pivot.

Assessing the risks and benefits of each pivot option is an essential step in determining the best strategy for your business. It is important to carefully evaluate the potential risks and benefits associated with each option before making a final decision.

When assessing the risks, consider the potential impact on revenue, market share, and brand reputation. For example, entering a new market may involve significant upfront costs, and there is a risk that the new market may not be profitable. Similarly, launching a new product may require significant investment in research and development, and there is a risk that the product may not be successful in the market.

On the other hand, there are also potential benefits associated with each pivot option. Entering a new market may provide new revenue streams and help diversify your business. Launching a new product may help you stay competitive in the market and attract new customers.

To evaluate the risks and benefits of each option, it may be helpful to develop a risk-benefit matrix. This tool can help you weigh the potential benefits against the potential risks and make a more informed decision.

Ultimately, the goal is to identify the pivot option that offers the best balance of potential benefits and acceptable risks for your business.

Consider the impact on stakeholders: When considering different pivot options, it is important to take into account the impact on stakeholders such as employees, customers, and partners. Any pivot option that involves significant changes to your business model, products or services, or operations can potentially have a significant impact on these stakeholders.

For employees, a pivot may require new skills or training, changes in roles and responsibilities, or even job loss in some cases. It is important to consider the potential impact on employees and develop a plan to mitigate any negative consequences. This may involve offering training or re-skilling opportunities, providing support for those who may be affected by job loss, or communicating the reasons and benefits of the pivot to employees to ensure their buy-in and support.

For customers, a pivot may affect their experience with your company or the products and services they rely on. It is important to consider how the pivot may impact your customers and develop a plan to minimize any negative impact. This may involve communicating the changes to customers in a clear and transparent way, providing support and resources to help them adapt to the changes, or even soliciting feedback from customers to ensure their needs are being met.

For partners and other stakeholders, a pivot may require changes in the way you work with them or even the termination of certain partnerships. It is important to consider the potential impact on these stakeholders and develop a plan to manage these relationships in a way that minimizes any negative impact. This may involve communicating the changes in a clear and transparent way, offering support and resources to help partners adapt to the changes, or even negotiating new partnerships that are better aligned with your new business strategy.

Overall, it is important to consider the impact of each pivot option on all stakeholders and develop a plan to manage the potential risks and challenges. By doing so, you can ensure that your pivot is successful and sustainable in the long run.

Choosing the best pivot option can be a challenging decision, as it requires weighing multiple factors and potential outcomes. Here are some key considerations to help you make the best choice:

➢ **Alignment with business goals:** Ensure that the pivot option aligns with your overall business goals and objectives. This will help ensure that the pivot is not just a short-term fix, but rather a strategic move that will help your business succeed in the long term.

➢ **Feasibility and resource requirements:** Consider the feasibility of each pivot option and the resources required to execute it. Will you need to hire new employees, invest in new technology, or partner with other businesses? Make sure that you have the resources available to support the pivot.

➢ **Potential return on investment:** Evaluate the potential return on investment for each pivot option. Will the pivot option result in increased revenue, market share, or profitability? Make sure that the potential benefits outweigh the costs.

➢ **Risk and impact on stakeholders:** Assess the risks associated with each pivot option and consider the impact on your employees, customers, and other stakeholders. Will the pivot option require significant changes in your organization or affect the customer experience? Make sure that the benefits of the pivot outweigh any potential negative impact on stakeholders.

> ➤ **Flexibility and adaptability:** Choose a pivot option that allows for flexibility and adaptability. Markets and industries are constantly changing, so it's important to choose a pivot option that can evolve with the market and adapt to changing conditions.

Once you have chosen the best pivot option, develop a detailed plan for executing the pivot. This should include specific timelines, milestones, and key performance indicators (KPIs) to track progress. Make sure to communicate the pivot plan to all stakeholders, including employees, customers, and investors, to ensure that everyone is aligned and supportive of the pivot.

Communicating the pivot to stakeholders is a crucial step in ensuring a successful transition. It's important to keep everyone informed and engaged throughout the process. Here are some strategies for effectively communicating the pivot:

> ➤ **Be transparent:** It's important to be open and honest about the reasons for the pivot, the changes being made, and the potential impact on stakeholders. Address any concerns or questions upfront and provide regular updates on progress.

> ➤ **Develop a communication plan:** Develop a clear communication plan that outlines the key messages, target audience, and communication channels to be used. This will help ensure that everyone receives the information they need in a timely and effective manner.

> ➤ **Tailor the message to the audience:** Different stakeholders will have different interests and concerns. Tailor the message to each audience to ensure that the information is relevant and meaningful.

> ➤ **Use a variety of communication channels:** Use a variety of communication channels, such as email, social media, and in-person meetings, to reach stakeholders. This will ensure that everyone has the opportunity to receive

the message in a way that works for them.

➢ **Address concerns and questions:** Be prepared to address any concerns or questions that stakeholders may have. This may involve holding Q&A sessions, providing additional resources, or connecting stakeholders with relevant contacts.

➢ **Celebrate successes:** As the pivot progresses, be sure to celebrate successes and milestones with stakeholders. This will help keep everyone engaged and motivated to see the pivot through to completion.

Monitoring and adjusting your pivot strategy is a critical step in ensuring its success. Here are some tips for effectively monitoring and adjusting your strategy:

➢ **Set up a system for tracking progress:** Establish a system for regularly tracking progress against your KPIs. This can be done through regular check-ins, meetings, or reports. Use this data to identify areas where the pivot strategy may need to be adjusted.

➢ **Stay up-to-date with market trends:** Keep a close eye on market trends and shifts in consumer behavior. This can help you identify potential threats or opportunities, and adjust your strategy accordingly.

➢ **Solicit feedback from stakeholders:** Regularly seek feedback from employees, customers, and other stakeholders. This can provide valuable insights into how the pivot is being perceived and what adjustments may be needed.

➢ **Remain flexible:** Be prepared to adjust your pivot strategy as needed. This may involve shifting resources, changing timelines, or adjusting your approach altogether.

➢ **Revisit your plan regularly:** Revisit your pivot plan

regularly to ensure it remains relevant and aligned with your business goals and objectives. This may involve updating your KPIs or adjusting your timeline based on new information.

Change can be difficult for individuals and organizations, and it is common for stakeholders to resist change. Overcoming resistance to change and getting buy-in from stakeholders requires a deliberate and strategic approach. Here are some strategies to consider:

Communicate the need for change: It's important to clearly communicate why change is necessary and the benefits it will bring. Be transparent about the reasons for the change, and explain how it aligns with the organization's goals and values.

Here are some key strategies for effective communication:

➢ **Be transparent:** Be open and honest about the reasons for the change. Explain how the current situation is not sustainable and how the proposed change will address the issue.

➢ **Provide context:** Give stakeholders the context and background they need to understand the change. This can include data, market trends, and other relevant information.

➢ **Explain the benefits:** Clearly articulate the benefits that the change will bring. Explain how it will improve the organization's performance, competitiveness, or ability to meet customer needs.

➢ **Address concerns:** Be prepared to address any concerns or objections that stakeholders may have. Acknowledge their concerns and provide evidence to support the need for change.

➢ **Invite feedback:** Encourage stakeholders to share their thoughts and feedback on the proposed change. This will help to build trust and engagement, and can also help to identify potential issues or challenges.

➤ **Provide support:** Offer resources and support to help stakeholders navigate the change. This can include training, coaching, or other resources to help them adapt to new roles, processes, or technologies.

➤ **Follow up:** Stay engaged with stakeholders throughout the change process, and provide regular updates on progress. This will help to build trust and maintain momentum towards the desired outcome.

Addressing concerns and objections is a crucial step in getting buy-in from stakeholders. When introducing change, it's common for stakeholders to have questions, concerns, or objections. It's important to listen to these concerns and address them thoughtfully, as ignoring or dismissing them can lead to resistance to the change.

One approach to addressing concerns and objections is to schedule one-on-one meetings with stakeholders to discuss their specific concerns. This allows for a more personalized approach and shows that you are taking their concerns seriously. During these meetings, it's important to actively listen and ask clarifying questions to fully understand their perspective.

Once you understand their concerns, it's important to address them directly and honestly. Be transparent about any limitations or challenges associated with the change, and explain how you plan to mitigate these risks. It may also be helpful to provide examples or data to support your argument.

Another approach is to hold town hall meetings or other group discussions to address common concerns and objections. This can be an effective way to address concerns in a more public forum, while also allowing stakeholders to hear from others who may have similar concerns.

In addition to addressing concerns and objections, it's important to emphasize the benefits of the change and how it aligns with the organization's goals and values. This can help stakeholders understand the importance of the change and feel more invested in its success.

Involving stakeholders in the change process is a crucial step in gaining their buy-in and commitment to the change. Here are some ways to involve stakeholders in the process:

➢ **Solicit feedback and ideas:** Ask stakeholders for their input and ideas on the change. This shows that their opinions are valued and can help identify potential issues and opportunities that may have been overlooked.

➢ **Involve stakeholders in decision-making:** If possible, involve stakeholders in the decision-making process. This could involve forming a committee or task force that includes representatives from different stakeholder groups.

➢ **Provide training and support:** Provide training and support to stakeholders to help them adapt to the change. This could involve offering workshops, training sessions, or one-on-one coaching.

➢ **Communicate regularly:** Keep stakeholders informed about the change process and progress. This could involve regular updates through email, meetings, or newsletters.

➢ **Recognize and reward participation:** Recognize and reward stakeholders who participate in the change process. This could involve providing incentives or recognition for their contributions.

Providing training and support is a critical component of overcoming resistance to change and getting buy-in from stakeholders. It can help stakeholders understand the changes being made and build the skills and confidence needed to succeed in the new environment. Here are some tips for providing effective training and support:

➢ **Identify training needs:** Conduct a thorough assessment of the skills and knowledge required to successfully implement the change. This will help you identify any gaps that need to be addressed through training and support.

➢ **Develop a training plan:** Based on the training needs assessment, develop a comprehensive training plan that outlines the training objectives, curriculum, delivery method, and schedule.

➢ **Provide ongoing support:** Offer ongoing support to help stakeholders adapt to the change. This could include offering coaching or mentoring, providing access to job aids or resources, or establishing a help desk to address questions or concerns.

➢ **Communicate the benefits:** Clearly communicate the benefits of the change and how the training and support will help stakeholders achieve their goals. This will help motivate them to engage in the training and apply what they have learned.

➢ **Offer incentives:** Consider offering incentives to encourage participation in the training and support programs. This could include recognition, bonuses, or other rewards.

➢ **Evaluate effectiveness:** Continuously evaluate the effectiveness of the training and support programs to ensure they are meeting the needs of stakeholders and helping them achieve their goals. Use feedback and evaluation data to make adjustments as needed.

Celebrating successes and milestones is an important aspect of overcoming resistance to change and getting buy-in from stakeholders. Here are some ways to celebrate successes and milestones:

➢ **Share progress updates:** Regularly share updates on the progress of the change effort. Communicate how the change is benefiting the organization, and celebrate milestones and successes along the way. This will keep stakeholders engaged and motivated.

➢ **Recognize individuals and teams:** Recognize individuals and teams for their contributions to the change effort. This could include giving awards or certificates, highlighting successes in meetings or newsletters, or acknowledging contributions in performance evaluations.

➢ **Hold events:** Hold events to celebrate successes and milestones. This could include a team lunch, a happy hour, or a more formal ceremony. Use these events to recognize individuals and teams, and to reinforce the importance of the change effort.

➢ **Create a culture of celebration:** Create a culture of celebration by encouraging individuals and teams to celebrate successes and milestones on their own. This could include creating a recognition program or establishing a "brag board" where individuals can share their successes.

➢ **Link celebrations to business results:** Link celebrations to business results to reinforce the importance of the change effort. For example, if the change effort has led to an increase in revenue, celebrate the success and reinforce the importance of the change effort in achieving that success.

Leading by example is a crucial aspect of overcoming resistance to change and getting buy-in from stakeholders. Here are some ways in which leaders can model the desired behaviors and attitudes:

➢ **Be visible and accessible:** Leaders should be visible and accessible to stakeholders during the change process. This includes being present and available to answer questions, address concerns, and provide support.

> **Communicate regularly:** Communication is key during times of change. Leaders should communicate regularly with stakeholders to provide updates on the progress of the change effort, address concerns and objections, and celebrate successes and milestones.

> **Provide support and resources:** Leaders should provide stakeholders with the support and resources they need to adapt to the change. This may include training, coaching, or counseling, as well as tools and technologies to help stakeholders be successful in their roles.

> **Demonstrate commitment:** Leaders should demonstrate their commitment to the change effort through their actions and behaviors. This includes being willing to make difficult decisions, taking accountability for the success of the change effort, and modeling the desired behaviors and attitudes.

> **Encourage and empower others:** Leaders should encourage and empower stakeholders to take ownership of the change effort and contribute their ideas and feedback. This helps to build buy-in and commitment to the change effort, and can lead to more successful outcomes.

A few examples of successful pivots and the lessons learned from them:

> **Netflix:** Netflix was originally a DVD rental service but pivoted to an online streaming service in the mid-2000s. The company's leadership realized that the future of media consumption was moving toward online streaming and invested heavily in developing a robust streaming platform. The pivot was successful, and Netflix has since become one of the largest streaming services in the world.

Lessons learned:

- ✓ Stay ahead of market trends and anticipate future changes

- ✓ Invest in technology and innovation

- ✓ Be willing to take risks and make bold moves

➢ **Slack:** Slack began as a gaming company but pivoted to become a communication platform for businesses. The company's leadership recognized that there was a gap in the market for a messaging platform specifically designed for teams and businesses, and pivoted to fill that need. The pivot was successful, and Slack has become a widely used communication tool in the workplace.

Lessons learned:

- ✓ Pay attention to market gaps and unmet needs

- ✓ Be willing to pivot and change direction when necessary

- ✓ Focus on providing a valuable solution to a specific problem

➢ **Twitter:** Twitter began as a podcasting company but pivoted to become a social media platform. The company's leadership realized that the future of communication was moving toward short, concise messages, and pivoted to create a platform that allowed users to share brief updates in real-time. The pivot was successful, and Twitter has become a major player in the social media landscape.

Lessons learned:

✓ Stay attuned to changes in communication and media consumption

✓ Focus on simplicity and ease-of-use

✓ Be willing to experiment and try new things

These examples demonstrate that successful pivots require a willingness to take risks, anticipate market changes, and adapt to new circumstances. By focusing on the needs of customers, investing in technology and innovation, and being willing to change direction when necessary, companies can pivot successfully and thrive in the long term.

Chapter 5: Leveraging Your Strengths and Assets

Identifying and leveraging your unique strengths and assets can give your business a competitive advantage and help you stand out in the marketplace. Here are some steps you can take to identify and leverage your unique strengths and assets:

Identifying your core competencies is a critical first step in leveraging your unique strengths and assets. Here are some steps you can take to identify your core competencies:

> **Analyze your business processes:** Start by analyzing your business processes and identifying the key activities that contribute to your success. For example, if you're a software company, your core competencies might include software development, testing, and deployment.

> **Identify your unique skills and knowledge:** Consider the skills and knowledge that set you apart from your competitors. These could include specialized expertise in a particular technology, a deep understanding of your target market, or unique insights into customer needs.

> **Assess your resources:** Assess your resources, including your physical assets, financial resources, and intellectual property. Consider how these resources contribute to your competitive advantage and how you can leverage them to drive growth.

> **Conduct a SWOT analysis:** Conduct a SWOT analysis to identify your strengths, weaknesses, opportunities, and threats. Use this analysis to identify your core competencies and the areas where you have a competitive advantage.

> **Gather feedback from customers and stakeholders:** Gather feedback from customers, suppliers, and other stakeholders to gain insights into your unique strengths and assets. This feedback can help you identify areas where you excel and areas where you may need to improve.

Once you have identified your core competencies, you can leverage them to drive growth and build a competitive advantage. Here are some ways to leverage your unique strengths and assets:

➢ **Focus on your strengths:** Identify the areas where you have a competitive advantage and focus your resources on these areas. This will help you differentiate yourself from your competitors and build a strong position in the market.

➢ **Develop new products and services:** Use your core competencies to develop new products and services that meet the needs of your target market. This will help you expand your business and reach new customers.

➢ **Partner with other businesses:** Partner with other businesses that complement your core competencies. This can help you access new markets and leverage your strengths to drive growth.

➢ **Build a strong brand:** Use your unique strengths and assets to build a strong brand that resonates with your target market. This will help you differentiate yourself from your competitors and build customer loyalty.

Assessing your resources is a crucial step in identifying and leveraging your unique strengths and assets. Resources include financial, human, and technological resources, among others. Here are some ways to assess your resources:

➢ **Financial resources:** Determine your business's financial health by analyzing your revenue, cash flow, and profits. Identify areas where you can reduce expenses and increase revenue to free up resources for growth initiatives.

➢ **Human resources:** Assess your team's skills, knowledge, and experience. Identify areas where you need to hire or develop talent to build the competencies necessary for growth. Consider outsourcing or partnering with other businesses to access specialized skills or expertise.

➤ **Technological resources:** Determine the technology and systems your business uses and how they contribute to your competitive advantage. Identify areas where you need to upgrade or invest in new technology to improve efficiencies and create new opportunities.

➤ **Intellectual property:** Identify any patents, trademarks, or other intellectual property that your business owns. Determine how you can leverage these assets to create new products or services or generate licensing revenue.

➤ **Brand reputation:** Assess your business's brand reputation and identify ways to enhance it. Determine how your brand can be leveraged to differentiate your business from competitors and create new opportunities.

Identifying your key customers is essential to understanding what sets your business apart from competitors and leveraging your strengths and assets. Here are some steps to help you identify your key customers:

➤ **Analyze your customer data:** Look at your sales data to identify which customers are bringing in the most revenue and which ones are most loyal. Identify common characteristics of these customers, such as demographics, industry, or geography.

➤ **Conduct customer surveys:** Ask your customers about their experience with your business, what they value most, and what they think sets you apart from competitors. This feedback can help you identify your unique strengths and assets.

➤ **Look at your competition:** Analyze your competitors and identify what sets your business apart from theirs. Consider what types of customers your competitors are targeting and whether there are opportunities to focus on a different niche.

> **Consider market trends:** Look at broader market trends to identify which customer segments are growing or shrinking. This can help you identify new opportunities to target customers with specific needs.

Understanding your industry is a crucial step in identifying and leveraging your unique strengths and assets. Here are some ways to gain a deeper understanding of your industry:

> **Research and analyze industry data:** Look for data and reports on your industry, including market trends, customer behavior, and competition. This information can help you identify opportunities and potential threats to your business.

> **Attend industry events:** Attend trade shows, conferences, and other industry events to network with other professionals and learn about the latest developments in your field.

> **Join industry associations:** Joining industry associations and organizations can provide you with access to valuable resources and opportunities to connect with other professionals in your industry.

> **Conduct customer research:** Conduct surveys and focus groups to gain insights into your customers' needs, preferences, and behaviors. This information can help you identify ways to better serve your customers and stand out from the competition.

> **Analyze your competitors:** Analyze your competitors' strengths and weaknesses, and identify ways you can differentiate your business and stand out in the market.

Leverage your brand: Your brand is a valuable asset that can help differentiate your business from competitors. Develop a strong brand identity and use it to communicate your unique value proposition to customers.

Here are some tips for leveraging your brand:

> **Develop a strong brand identity:** Your brand identity is more than just your logo and color scheme. It's the personality and values that your brand represents. Develop a clear and consistent brand identity that resonates with your target audience.

> **Consistently communicate your brand:** Your brand should be communicated consistently across all touchpoints, including your website, social media channels, and marketing materials. Make sure your messaging and visuals are in line with your brand identity.

> **Focus on your unique value proposition:** Identify what makes your business unique and communicate that to your customers. This could be your exceptional customer service, high-quality products, or competitive pricing.

> **Use social media to your advantage:** Social media is a powerful tool for building your brand and engaging with your audience. Use social media platforms to share your brand story, showcase your products, and connect with customers.

> **Leverage customer feedback:** Listen to customer feedback and use it to improve your brand. Address any negative feedback promptly and use positive feedback to reinforce your brand messaging.

Building strategic partnerships is a key way to leverage your strengths and assets to achieve greater success. Here are some steps you can take to build these partnerships:

> **Identify potential partners:** Look for businesses or organizations that share your values and goals or can

provide complementary products or services.

➢ **Research potential partners:** Research the potential partners to learn more about their business and their strengths and weaknesses. This information can help you determine if they are a good fit for your business.

➢ **Reach out to potential partners:** Once you have identified potential partners, reach out to them to start a conversation about a possible partnership. This could include setting up a meeting, sending an email, or making a phone call.

➢ **Develop a partnership plan:** Work with your potential partner to develop a partnership plan that outlines the goals, objectives, and expected outcomes of the partnership.

➢ **Determine the terms of the partnership:** Once you have developed a partnership plan, determine the terms of the partnership, including the roles and responsibilities of each partner, the resources required, and how success will be measured.

➢ **Implement the partnership plan:** Once the partnership plan is in place, implement it according to the agreed-upon terms. Monitor progress regularly and make adjustments as needed.

➢ **Celebrate success:** Celebrate successes and milestones along the way to keep both partners engaged and motivated.

Be willing to innovate:
Innovation can help you stay ahead of the competition, and leveraging your unique strengths and assets is key to successful innovation. Here are some ways to be willing to innovate:

➢ **Foster a culture of innovation:** Encourage creativity and experimentation among your team members. Create an environment that is supportive of new ideas and is open to trying new things.

> **Stay informed:** Keep up-to-date with the latest trends and developments in your industry. Attend conferences, workshops, and other events to learn about emerging technologies, techniques, and strategies.

> **Look for inspiration:** Seek inspiration from other industries, businesses, or organizations. Look for innovative ideas that could be adapted to your business.

> **Experiment:** Be willing to try new things and experiment with new ideas. Test new products, services, or business models on a small scale before committing to a full-scale rollout.

> **Be open to feedback:** Listen to feedback from customers, employees, and other stakeholders. Use their insights to refine and improve your innovation efforts.

> **Focus on value:** Keep the customer at the center of your innovation efforts. Focus on creating value for them by solving their problems, meeting their needs, or providing them with new experiences.

> **Measure success:** Establish clear metrics to measure the success of your innovation efforts. Monitor progress regularly and be willing to adjust your approach based on the data.

Developing innovative products and services that meet evolving customer needs is essential to staying competitive in today's rapidly changing business landscape. Here are some techniques that can help:

> **Conduct market research:** Start by conducting market research to gain insights into customer needs, preferences, and behavior. This can include surveys, focus groups, and

interviews. Use the information gathered to identify gaps in the market and potential opportunities for innovation.

➢ **Foster a culture of innovation:** Encourage employees to share ideas and be creative. Reward innovation and risk-taking, and create a culture that values experimentation and learning from failure.

➢ **Use design thinking:** Design thinking is a user-centered approach to innovation that involves empathy, creativity, and experimentation. Use design thinking to develop a deep understanding of customer needs and pain points, and to generate ideas for innovative products and services.

➢ **Collaborate with customers:** Collaborate with customers to co-create products and services that meet their needs. This can include involving customers in the design process, gathering feedback on prototypes, and testing products and services in real-world settings.

➢ **Use agile development methodologies:** Agile development methodologies involve rapid prototyping, iterative testing, and continuous improvement. Use agile methodologies to quickly develop and test new products and services, and to make adjustments based on customer feedback.

➢ **Incorporate emerging technologies:** Keep up-to-date with emerging technologies and consider how they can be used to develop innovative products and services. This could include technologies such as artificial intelligence, blockchain, or virtual and augmented reality.

➢ **Stay competitive:** Keep a close eye on your competitors and the broader market to identify emerging trends and new opportunities for innovation. Be willing to adapt and evolve your products and services to stay ahead of the curve.

Creating a culture of innovation and experimentation can be challenging, but it is essential for businesses that want to stay competitive and adapt to changing market conditions. Here are some tips for fostering a culture of innovation in your organization:

➢ **Encourage creativity:** Encourage your employees to be creative and think outside the box. Provide opportunities for brainstorming and idea-sharing sessions, and celebrate new ideas and innovative solutions.

➢ **Empower your employees:** Empower your employees to take risks and experiment with new ideas. Provide them with the resources and support they need to pursue new initiatives and projects.

➢ **Foster a learning mindset:** Encourage a culture of continuous learning and growth. Provide opportunities for professional development and training, and reward employees who take the initiative to learn new skills and take on new challenges.

➢ **Embrace failure:** Encourage a culture where failure is seen as an opportunity to learn and grow. Celebrate the lessons learned from failures and encourage employees to take risks and learn from their mistakes.

➢ **Create a supportive environment:** Foster a supportive work environment where employees feel comfortable sharing their ideas and feedback. Encourage collaboration and open communication, and provide regular opportunities for feedback and discussion.

➢ **Reward innovation:** Reward and recognize employees who demonstrate a commitment to innovation and experimentation. Offer incentives and bonuses for successful innovation projects, and celebrate the achievements of your employees and teams.

➢ **Lead by example:** Set an example for your employees by

embracing innovation and experimentation in your own work. Encourage your managers and leaders to model the behaviors and attitudes you want to see in your organization.

Chapter 6: Navigating Turbulent Times

In today's business environment, it's essential to stay resilient in the face of uncertainty and change. Here are some tips on how to build resilience and thrive in challenging times:

Stay positive: It's important to maintain a positive attitude and outlook, even in the face of adversity. Look for the silver lining in every situation and focus on the opportunities that exist rather than the challenges.

Maintaining a positive attitude can help individuals and businesses stay resilient in the face of uncertainty and change. Here are some tips for staying positive:

➢ **Practice gratitude:** Take time each day to reflect on the things you're grateful for, no matter how small they may seem. This can help shift your focus from what you don't have to what you do have.

➢ **Surround yourself with positivity:** Spend time with people who uplift and support you. This could be friends, family, or colleagues who share your values and goals.

➢ **Practice self-care:** Taking care of your physical and emotional well-being can help you stay grounded and resilient. This could include getting enough sleep, eating healthy, exercising, and engaging in activities that bring you joy.

➢ **Stay informed, but limit exposure to negative news:** It's important to stay informed about what's happening in the world, but consuming too much negative news can be overwhelming and draining. Set limits on how much news you consume each day.

➢ **Focus on what you can control:** There are many things in life that are beyond our control, but focusing on what you can control can help you feel empowered and proactive.

➢ **Embrace change as an opportunity for growth:** Change can be uncomfortable, but it also presents opportunities for learning and growth. Embrace new experiences and challenges with a growth mindset, and view setbacks as opportunities to learn and improve.

➢ **Celebrate small wins:** Take time to acknowledge and celebrate small wins and accomplishments along the way. This can help boost morale and keep you motivated during times of uncertainty and change.

Be adaptable: Be prepared to adapt to changing circumstances and be open to new ideas and approaches. This may require stepping outside of your comfort zone and taking calculated risks.

Being adaptable is a key trait of resilience. The ability to pivot and adjust course when faced with unexpected challenges or opportunities can be the difference between success and failure. Here are some tips for being more adaptable:

➢ **Embrace change:** Rather than resisting change, approach it with an open mind and a willingness to learn and grow. Recognize that change can bring new opportunities and experiences.

➢ **Stay curious:** Ask questions and seek out new information and perspectives. This can help you stay ahead of the curve and anticipate changes before they happen.

➢ **Build a strong network:** Surround yourself with people who have diverse skills, knowledge, and experiences. This can provide you with a range of perspectives and resources to draw from when faced with unexpected challenges.

➢ **Develop new skills:** Continuously learning and developing new skills can help you adapt to changing circumstances and stay ahead of the curve.

> **Practice resilience:** Resilience is a skill that can be developed and strengthened over time. By practicing resilience in small ways, such as taking on new challenges or overcoming obstacles, you can build your capacity to handle bigger challenges in the future.

Focus on your strengths: Identify your strengths and leverage them to your advantage. This will help you build confidence and resilience and enable you to overcome obstacles more effectively.

Focusing on your strengths can help you stay resilient in the face of uncertainty and change. Here are some ways to do that:

> **Identify your strengths:** Take some time to reflect on your past successes and identify the strengths that helped you achieve them. Consider asking colleagues or friends for feedback on your strengths as well.

> **Leverage your strengths:** Once you have identified your strengths, find ways to leverage them in your work and personal life. This can help you build confidence and a sense of purpose, which can in turn help you stay resilient in the face of challenges.

> **Build on your strengths:** Continue to develop and improve your strengths over time. Seek out opportunities to learn new skills or deepen your existing knowledge, and look for ways to apply your strengths in new and different contexts.

> **Surround yourself with support:** Surround yourself with people who believe in you and support your strengths. This can be a team of colleagues, friends, or family members who can offer encouragement and help you stay motivated.

> **Stay positive:** Maintaining a positive attitude can help you

stay resilient in the face of challenges. Look for the good in every situation, and focus on what you can do to move forward rather than dwelling on the negative.

Build a support network: Surround yourself with people who can provide support and guidance during challenging times. This may include mentors, coaches, colleagues, or family and friends.

Building a support network is important for staying resilient in the face of uncertainty and change. Here are some tips:

> **Identify potential sources of support:** Make a list of people who you trust and who have a positive impact on your life. This may include friends, family members, colleagues, or mentors.

> **Reach out for help:** Don't be afraid to ask for help when you need it. Reach out to your support network and let them know what you're going through. They may be able to offer advice, resources, or simply a listening ear.

> **Cultivate positive relationships:** Invest in your relationships with the people in your support network. Make time for them, express gratitude, and be willing to reciprocate when they need support.

> **Join a community or group:** Consider joining a group or community of people who share your interests or experiences. This can provide a sense of belonging and connection, and may offer opportunities for learning and growth.

> **Seek professional help:** If you're struggling with mental health issues or other challenges that require professional support, don't hesitate to seek help from a therapist, counselor, or other healthcare provider.

Practice self-care: Take care of yourself physically, mentally, and emotionally. This may involve engaging in regular exercise, eating a healthy diet, getting enough sleep, and taking time for relaxation and stress management.

Taking care of yourself is an important aspect of staying resilient in the face of uncertainty and change. Here are some tips for practicing self-care:

➤ **Exercise regularly:** Exercise is a great way to manage stress, improve mood, and boost overall health. Aim for at least 30 minutes of physical activity each day, whether it's going for a walk, practicing yoga, or hitting the gym.

➤ **Eat a healthy diet:** A nutritious, well-balanced diet can help improve energy levels, mood, and overall health. Focus on eating a variety of whole foods, including fruits, vegetables, lean proteins, and healthy fats.

➤ **Get enough sleep:** Lack of sleep can make it difficult to cope with stress and stay resilient. Aim for 7-8 hours of sleep each night, and establish a consistent sleep schedule.

➤ **Practice relaxation techniques:** Incorporate relaxation techniques into your daily routine to help manage stress and promote mental and emotional well-being. This could include practices like deep breathing, meditation, or mindfulness exercises.

➤ **Connect with others:** Building and maintaining strong social connections can help provide a sense of support and belonging, which can be especially important during times of uncertainty and change.

➤ **Engage in hobbies and activities you enjoy:** Make time for activities that bring you joy and help you recharge. This could include hobbies like painting, reading, or gardening, or participating in sports or other recreational activities.

Learn from failure: Failure is a natural part of the learning process. Don't be afraid to take risks and make mistakes, but be sure to learn from them and use them as opportunities for growth and development.

Learning from failure is essential to staying resilient in the face of uncertainty and change. Here are some tips for learning from failure:

> **Analyze the situation:** Take time to reflect on what happened and why it didn't go as planned. Identify any mistakes or missteps that may have contributed to the failure.

> **Seek feedback:** Ask for feedback from others involved in the situation, as well as those who may have observed from the outside. This can help you gain a different perspective and identify areas for improvement.

> **Reframe the situation:** Instead of viewing the situation as a failure, try to reframe it as a learning opportunity. What did you learn? How can you apply this knowledge in the future?

> **Take action:** Use what you learned to make changes and improvements for the future. This could involve adjusting your approach, seeking additional training or resources, or simply trying again with a different strategy.

> **Practice resilience:** Remember that failure is not the end of the road. Stay positive, keep an open mind, and be willing to adapt and persevere in the face of setbacks.

Stay focused on your goals: Keep your eyes on the prize and stay focused on your goals, even when the road ahead is rocky. This will help you maintain a sense of purpose and direction and give you the motivation you need to keep moving forward.

Staying focused on your goals is essential for building resilience in the face of uncertainty and change. It's easy to get distracted by the challenges and obstacles that arise along the way, but it's important to keep your eyes on the prize and remain committed to your objectives. Here are some tips for staying focused on your goals:

> **Define your goals:** Clearly define your short-term and long-term goals and make sure they are realistic, measurable, and achievable. Write them down and review them regularly to keep them top of mind.

> **Break them down:** Break your goals down into smaller, manageable steps. This will make them less overwhelming and easier to achieve. Create a timeline for each step and set deadlines to keep yourself accountable.

> **Prioritize:** Identify the most important tasks and focus on completing them first. This will help you make progress and build momentum towards your larger goals.

> **Stay organized:** Use tools like calendars, to-do lists, and project management software to stay organized and keep track of your progress. This will help you stay on track and avoid getting sidetracked by other tasks.

> **Celebrate successes:** Celebrate your successes and milestones along the way. This will help you stay motivated and inspired to keep working towards your goals.

> **Stay motivated:** Find ways to stay motivated and inspired. This could involve reading books, watching videos, listening to podcasts, or attending events related to your goals.

> **Get support:** Surround yourself with people who support and encourage you. This could be friends, family, mentors, or a coach. Having a support system can help you stay focused and motivated, especially during challenging times.

In summary, staying resilient in the face of uncertainty and change requires a positive attitude, adaptability, a focus on strengths, a support network, self-care, learning from failure, and a focus on goals. By incorporating these tips into your daily life, you can build the resilience you need to thrive in today's dynamic business environment.

In today's fast-paced business environment, it's essential to be able to manage risk and adapt to unexpected challenges. Here are some strategies for doing so:

Conducting a risk assessment is an important first step in managing risk and adapting to unexpected challenges. To do this, you should identify potential risks that could impact your business, such as changes in the market, natural disasters, or cyber-attacks.

Once you have identified potential risks, assess their likelihood and potential impact on your business. This will help you prioritize your risks and develop strategies to mitigate them. For example, if a natural disaster is likely to occur, you may need to develop a contingency plan to ensure that your business can continue to operate even if your physical location is damaged or inaccessible.

It's important to regularly review and update your risk assessment as your business evolves and as new risks emerge. This will help you stay prepared for unexpected challenges and minimize their impact on your business.

Some additional strategies for managing risk and adapting to unexpected challenges include:

> **Develop contingency plans:** Develop plans for how your business will respond to unexpected events, such as a sudden loss of revenue or a key employee leaving. Make sure these plans are clearly documented and communicated to all relevant stakeholders.

> **Diversify your revenue streams:** Relying on one product or service for all of your revenue can be risky. Look for

opportunities to diversify your revenue streams to reduce your risk.

➢ **Build strong relationships with suppliers and partners:** Strong relationships with suppliers and partners can help you navigate unexpected challenges, such as supply chain disruptions or unexpected changes in the market.

➢ **Maintain financial reserves:** Having financial reserves can help you weather unexpected challenges, such as a sudden drop in revenue or an unexpected expense.

➢ **Continuously monitor and evaluate:** Continuously monitor and evaluate your business to identify potential risks and opportunities for improvement. This will help you stay agile and adaptable in the face of unexpected challenges.

Developing a culture of risk management is crucial for businesses to be able to manage unexpected challenges and adapt to changing circumstances. Here are some strategies to help create a culture of risk management within your organization:

➢ **Promote open communication:** Encourage open and honest communication within your organization. Create an environment where employees feel comfortable reporting potential risks or issues without fear of retaliation. This can help identify potential risks early and prevent them from becoming larger problems.

➢ **Encourage employee involvement:** Involve employees in the risk management process by asking for their input and feedback. Employees who are closer to the day-to-day operations of the business may have insights into potential risks that management may not be aware of. Involving employees also helps to build a sense of ownership and accountability for managing risks.

➤ **Train employees on risk management:** Provide training to employees on risk management best practices and how to identify potential risks. This can help build a common language and understanding of risk management within your organization.

➤ **Regularly review and update risk management processes:** Regularly review and update your risk management processes to ensure they are effective and relevant. As your business evolves, so too may the risks it faces. Staying current and proactive in your risk management approach can help mitigate potential issues before they become major problems.

➤ **Lead by example:** As a leader, it's important to lead by example and demonstrate the importance of risk management. This means taking risks seriously, being proactive in identifying and mitigating risks, and ensuring that risk management is a priority within the organization.

Diversifying your revenue streams is a key strategy for managing risk and adapting to unexpected challenges in your business. When you rely on a single product or service for your revenue, you run the risk of being heavily impacted if there are any unexpected changes or disruptions in that market.

Here are some strategies to diversify your revenue streams:

➤ **Expand your product or service offerings:** Look for ways to expand your product or service offerings to reach new markets and customers. This could involve developing new products or services that complement your existing offerings or entering into new markets or industries.

➤ **Partner with other businesses:** Look for opportunities to partner with other businesses to offer joint products or services. This can help you reach new customers and expand your offerings without incurring significant costs.

➢ **Offer subscriptions or memberships:** Consider offering subscriptions or memberships to your products or services. This can provide you with a more predictable revenue stream and help you build a loyal customer base.

➢ **Develop a passive income stream:** Look for ways to generate passive income, such as through affiliate marketing or advertising. This can provide you with a steady stream of revenue without requiring significant ongoing effort.

➢ **Leverage your expertise:** Consider offering consulting or coaching services based on your expertise in your industry. This can provide you with a new revenue stream while also building your brand and reputation.

Staying informed is a crucial part of managing risk and adapting to unexpected challenges in business. It's important to keep up-to-date with the latest trends and developments in your industry, as well as any changes in the broader economic, political, or social environment that may impact your business. Here are some tips for staying informed:

➢ **Monitor industry news and publications:** Regularly read industry news sources and publications to stay up-to-date with the latest trends and developments in your field. This will help you identify potential opportunities and threats, and adjust your strategies accordingly.

➢ **Attend industry events and conferences:** Attend industry events and conferences to network with peers and gain insights into new technologies, products, and services that may impact your business.

➢ **Follow thought leaders and influencers:** Follow industry thought leaders and influencers on social media and subscribe to their blogs or newsletters to stay informed on the latest trends and best practices.

> **Join industry associations and groups:** Join industry associations and groups to connect with peers and stay informed on the latest trends and developments in your field.

> **Engage with customers and stakeholders:** Regularly engage with customers and stakeholders to gather feedback on your products and services, and stay informed on their changing needs and preferences.

> **Conduct market research:** Conduct regular market research to gather data on industry trends, customer needs, and competitor activities. This will help you stay ahead of the curve and identify potential opportunities and threats.

Being flexible is essential for managing risk and adapting to unexpected challenges in your business. Here are some strategies for building flexibility into your operations:

> **Foster a culture of flexibility:** Encourage open communication and collaboration within your organization to foster a culture that embraces change and adapts quickly to new circumstances.

> **Use agile methodologies:** Adopt agile methodologies in your product development process to allow for rapid iteration and adjustment in response to customer feedback and changing market conditions.

> **Keep an eye on the competition:** Monitor the activities of your competitors and be prepared to adjust your strategy to stay ahead of the curve.

> **Use data to make informed decisions:** Make data-driven decisions and use analytics to track the performance of your business and identify areas for

improvement.

> **Maintain a lean organization:** Avoid becoming overly bureaucratic or hierarchical, which can make it difficult to adapt quickly to new circumstances.

> **Stay in touch with your customers:** Keep your finger on the pulse of your customers' needs and preferences to ensure that you are providing the products and services they want.

Building a strong network is essential for managing risk and adapting to unexpected challenges in business. By connecting with other businesses, industry experts, and mentors, you can gain valuable insights and advice on how to navigate difficult situations.

Here are some tips for building a strong network:

> **Attend industry events and conferences:** Attend events and conferences in your industry to meet other professionals and stay up-to-date with the latest trends and developments.

> **Join industry groups and associations:** Join industry groups and associations to connect with other professionals and share best practices.

> **Participate in online forums and social media groups:** Participate in online forums and social media groups to connect with other professionals and stay informed about industry news and trends.

> **Seek out mentors and advisors:** Seek out mentors and advisors who can provide guidance and support as you navigate the challenges of running a business.

> **Collaborate with other businesses:** Collaborate with other businesses on projects or initiatives to build relationships and gain new perspectives.

Maintaining a strong financial position is essential for managing risks and adapting to unexpected challenges in business. Here are some strategies for keeping your business financially healthy:

➤ **Manage your cash flow:** Cash flow is the lifeblood of any business. Ensure that you have a clear understanding of your cash inflows and outflows and that you're managing your cash effectively. This involves monitoring your accounts receivable and payable, negotiating payment terms with suppliers and customers, and forecasting your cash flow to ensure that you have sufficient funds to cover your expenses.

➤ **Reduce your debt:** High levels of debt can make your business vulnerable to financial shocks. Aim to reduce your debt by paying down your loans and credit lines and avoiding taking on new debt unless it's necessary.

➤ **Build up your reserves:** Building up a reserve of cash and other liquid assets can provide a buffer against unexpected challenges such as a sudden drop in sales or an unexpected expense. Aim to build up a reserve of at least three to six months' worth of operating expenses.

➤ **Monitor your financial metrics:** Keep a close eye on your financial metrics such as revenue, profit margins, and return on investment. This will help you identify potential issues early on and take corrective action before they become more serious.

➤ **Seek professional advice:** Consider working with a financial advisor or accountant who can provide guidance on financial planning, risk management, and tax strategies. This can help you make informed decisions and avoid costly mistakes.

In today's fast-paced and constantly changing business

environment, agility and flexibility are critical factors in building a business that can withstand anything. Businesses that are agile and flexible can quickly adapt to changes in the market, customer preferences, and other external factors, which helps them stay ahead of the competition and thrive in uncertain times.

Here are some key ways agility and flexibility can help businesses build resilience:

Adapting to changing customer needs is a critical aspect of building a business that can withstand anything. With the rapid pace of technological change and increasing competition, businesses must be agile and flexible in responding to evolving customer needs and preferences.

One of the key ways businesses can adapt to changing customer needs is by actively seeking feedback from their customers. This can involve conducting surveys, focus groups, or individual customer interviews to gain insights into what customers want and need. By gathering this information, businesses can adjust their products and services to better meet customer expectations.

Another important factor is staying current with market trends and anticipating future customer needs. This can involve monitoring competitors, attending industry events, and analyzing customer data to identify emerging trends and preferences. By staying ahead of the curve, businesses can be proactive in responding to changing customer needs and developing new products and services that meet those needs.

In addition to being proactive, businesses must also be willing to make changes quickly when necessary. This means being flexible in terms of organizational structure, processes, and operations. For example, businesses may need to adjust their supply chain, marketing strategy, or customer service approach to meet changing customer needs.

Finally, businesses must be willing to take calculated risks in order to adapt and evolve. This may involve experimenting with new products or services, entering new markets, or trying out new marketing approaches. While there is always some degree of risk involved, businesses that are willing to take calculated risks are often the ones that reap the greatest rewards in terms of growth and profitability.

In summary, adapting to changing customer needs is a critical factor in building a business that can withstand anything. By seeking feedback, staying current with market trends, being flexible, and taking calculated risks, businesses can better meet customer expectations and stay ahead of the competition.

Responding to market changes: Market conditions can change rapidly, and businesses that are agile can quickly adjust their strategy and operations to take advantage of new opportunities or mitigate potential threats. This requires a willingness to experiment, take risks, and constantly evaluate the effectiveness of your approach.

Responding to market changes is crucial for businesses that want to remain competitive and relevant. Here are some strategies that can help businesses stay agile and adapt to market changes:

> **Monitor the market:** Keep an eye on industry trends, consumer behavior, and competitor activities to stay informed of changes in the market. This information can help you identify potential opportunities or threats and adjust your strategy accordingly.

> **Embrace new technology:** Technology is constantly evolving, and businesses that can adopt and leverage new tools and platforms are more likely to succeed. For example, businesses can use artificial intelligence (AI) and data analytics to gain insights into customer behavior and improve their products and services.

> **Foster a culture of innovation:** Encourage creativity and experimentation within your organization. This can help generate new ideas and approaches that can help you stay ahead of the curve and respond to market changes more

quickly.

> **Build strategic partnerships:** Collaborate with other businesses or organizations that share your values or can provide complementary products or services. These partnerships can help you leverage your strengths and assets to achieve greater success and respond to market changes more effectively.

> **Stay nimble:** Maintain a lean organizational structure and be prepared to make changes quickly. This can help you respond to market changes more rapidly and capitalize on new opportunities.

> **Focus on the customer:** Keep the customer at the center of everything you do. By listening to customer feedback and responding to their needs, you can stay ahead of the competition and adapt to market changes more effectively.

In today's fast-paced business environment, technology is playing an increasingly important role in driving innovation and growth. By embracing technology and adapting to new tools and platforms, businesses can improve efficiency, streamline operations, and enhance the customer experience.

One of the keys to success in this area is agility and flexibility. Businesses that are willing to experiment with new technologies and approaches can quickly identify what works and what doesn't, and make the necessary adjustments to stay ahead of the curve. This requires a willingness to take risks, be open to new ideas, and constantly evaluate the effectiveness of your approach.

There are a number of ways that businesses can embrace technology and stay ahead of the curve. For example, they can invest in new software and hardware solutions to improve productivity and streamline operations. They can also use data analytics and machine learning tools to better understand customer behavior and preferences, and develop more targeted and effective marketing strategies.

In addition, businesses can leverage emerging technologies such as artificial intelligence, virtual and augmented reality, and the Internet of Things (IoT) to create new products and services that meet evolving customer needs. These technologies can also help businesses develop more personalized and immersive customer experiences, which can help drive customer loyalty and satisfaction.

Of course, it's important to remember that technology is not a silver bullet solution. Businesses must also focus on developing strong relationships with their customers, maintaining a strong financial position, and building a culture of innovation and experimentation within their organization. By combining these elements with a willingness to embrace new technologies, businesses can build a resilient and adaptable business that can withstand anything.

Building a strong team is a critical aspect of building a business that can withstand anything. An agile and flexible team is one that is capable of quickly adapting to changing circumstances and responding to unexpected challenges. Here are some tips for building a strong and flexible team:

➢ **Hire for agility:** When building your team, look for candidates who are adaptable, open-minded, and willing to embrace change. These individuals are more likely to be able to quickly pivot and adjust to unexpected challenges.

➢ **Foster a culture of continuous learning:** Encourage your team to continually learn and develop new skills. Provide opportunities for training, mentorship, and professional development to ensure that your team is equipped with the knowledge and tools they need to succeed.

➢ **Promote collaboration and communication:** Strong communication and collaboration skills are essential for an agile and flexible team. Encourage your team to work together, share ideas, and communicate openly and honestly.

➢ **Empower your team:** Give your team the autonomy and authority they need to make decisions and take action. This will allow them to quickly respond to unexpected challenges without having to wait for approval or direction from upper management.

➢ **Embrace diversity:** A diverse team with a range of skills, perspectives, and backgrounds can bring fresh ideas and approaches to problem-solving. Encourage diversity and inclusion within your team to create a more innovative and agile organization.

➢ **Reward agility and flexibility:** Recognize and reward team members who demonstrate agility and flexibility in their work. This will encourage others to embrace these qualities and create a culture of resilience and adaptability.

By building a strong and flexible team, businesses can ensure that they are prepared to face any challenge that comes their way. With the right people, culture, and mindset, businesses can become more agile, responsive, and innovative, and ultimately build a sustainable and successful organization.

Being open to new ideas is crucial for building a business that can withstand anything. In today's fast-paced and rapidly changing world, businesses must be agile and flexible in order to adapt to new trends and technologies, as well as to respond to shifting customer needs and preferences.

To be open to new ideas, businesses must create a culture that encourages experimentation and innovation. This means empowering employees to take risks and try new things, as well as providing them with the resources and support they need to succeed.

One way to foster a culture of innovation is to establish cross-functional teams that bring together employees from different departments and backgrounds. This can encourage the exchange of ideas and perspectives, and help break down silos within the organization.

Another way to stay open to new ideas is to stay connected to the broader business community. This means attending industry events, networking with peers, and participating in online communities and forums where new trends and ideas are discussed.

Finally, businesses must be willing to invest in new technologies and processes that can help them stay ahead of the curve. This requires a willingness to experiment and take calculated risks, as well as a commitment to ongoing learning and development.

In conclusion, being open to new ideas is essential for building a business that can withstand anything. By fostering a culture of innovation, staying connected to the broader business community, and investing in new technologies and processes, businesses can stay ahead of the curve and navigate through uncertain times with confidence.

Chapter 7: Building a Culture of Continuous Innovation

Fostering a culture of experimentation, learning, and growth is essential for businesses to stay ahead of the curve and adapt to changing market conditions. Here are some strategies for building a culture that promotes experimentation, learning, and growth:

Encouraging open communication is essential to fostering a culture of experimentation, learning, and growth. When team members feel comfortable sharing their ideas and perspectives, it can lead to new insights and approaches that may have otherwise been overlooked.

To encourage open communication, it is important to create a safe and supportive environment where everyone feels comfortable sharing their thoughts and feedback. This can involve setting clear expectations around communication, providing opportunities for team members to share their ideas, and actively listening to and responding to their feedback.

One effective way to encourage open communication is to hold regular team meetings or brainstorming sessions where team members can share their ideas and collaborate on new projects. It is also important to provide opportunities for individual team members to share their thoughts and perspectives, such as through one-on-one meetings or feedback sessions.

Another key aspect of fostering open communication is to create a culture of psychological safety, where team members feel comfortable taking risks and making mistakes. This can involve acknowledging and learning from failures, celebrating successes, and promoting a growth mindset.

By fostering a culture of open communication, you can create a team that is more willing to experiment, learn, and grow. This can lead to more innovative ideas, better decision-making, and a stronger sense of collaboration and engagement among team members.

Celebrating both successes and failures, you can create a culture of experimentation, learning, and growth. Celebrating successes can motivate your team and reinforce the importance of hard work and dedication, while celebrating failures can help your team members learn from their mistakes and improve their skills.

When celebrating successes, be sure to acknowledge the contributions of your team members and recognize their hard work and dedication. This can be done through verbal recognition, awards, or other forms of recognition, such as bonuses or promotions.

When celebrating failures, it's important to focus on the learning opportunities that arise from these experiences. Encourage your team members to reflect on what went wrong and what they could have done differently. This can help them develop new skills and approaches and improve their performance in the future.

By celebrating both successes and failures, you can create a culture of experimentation, learning, and growth where your team members feel empowered to take risks, try new things, and continuously improve.

Providing opportunities for learning is a crucial component in fostering a culture of experimentation, learning, and growth within an organization. Employees who are given opportunities to learn and grow are more likely to be engaged, motivated, and committed to their work.

One way to provide learning opportunities is through formal training programs. These can include workshops, seminars, and courses that teach specific skills or knowledge related to the job. Providing access to these types of programs can help employees develop new skills and knowledge that they can apply to their work.

On-the-job learning experiences are also important. These can include giving employees opportunities to take on new projects or assignments that are outside of their comfort zone. By taking on new challenges, employees can develop new skills, gain experience, and grow professionally.

Mentoring programs are another way to provide learning

opportunities. Pairing employees with experienced mentors who can offer guidance and support can help employees develop new skills and gain valuable insights into the industry.

Finally, it's important to create a culture that values learning and growth. Leaders should model a commitment to learning by engaging in ongoing professional development and encouraging their team members to do the same. By creating a culture that values learning, employees will be more likely to seek out opportunities for growth and development, and the organization as a whole will be better positioned to adapt to new challenges and opportunities.

To foster a culture of experimentation, businesses should create an environment where taking risks and trying new things is encouraged and rewarded. Here are some ways to achieve this:

➢ **Encourage brainstorming:** Encourage your team to brainstorm ideas and concepts, even if they seem far-fetched or outside the box. Allow everyone to contribute and explore all possibilities without fear of judgment or criticism.

➢ **Start small:** Encourage your team to start with small experiments, testing out new ideas or approaches on a small scale before rolling them out more broadly. This can help mitigate the risks associated with trying something new.

➢ **Embrace failure:** Encourage your team to see failure as an opportunity to learn and grow, rather than something to be feared. Celebrate failures and use them as learning experiences to inform future experiments and decisions.

➢ **Provide resources and support:** Provide your team with the resources they need to conduct experiments and try new things. This can include time, funding, and access to tools and technology.

➢ **Recognize and reward success:** When experiments are

successful, recognize and reward the team members involved. This can be in the form of bonuses, promotions, or simply public recognition for their contributions.

Lead by example: As a leader, model the behaviors you want to see in your team. Be open to new ideas and perspectives, and encourage experimentation and learning. This can set the tone for your team and create a culture that promotes experimentation, learning, and growth.

Leading by example is a crucial aspect of fostering a culture of experimentation, learning, and growth. Here are a few ways you can lead by example:

➢ **Experiment yourself:** As a leader, you should also experiment and take calculated risks. This shows your team that you are willing to try new things and take responsibility for your actions.

➢ **Admit your mistakes:** No one is perfect, and mistakes are a part of learning. As a leader, you should admit your mistakes and take responsibility for them. This shows your team that it's okay to make mistakes and that you value honesty and transparency.

➢ **Encourage feedback:** As a leader, you should also seek feedback from your team and encourage them to provide honest feedback as well. This shows that you value their input and are willing to learn and grow.

➢ **Provide opportunities for growth:** Provide opportunities for your team to learn and grow, both through formal training programs and on-the-job experiences. This shows that you value their development and are invested in their success.

➢ **Celebrate successes and failures:** Celebrate both your team's successes and their failures. This shows that you value the learning process and encourage experimentation, even if it doesn't always lead to success.

Providing regular feedback is crucial for fostering a culture of experimentation, learning, and growth in any organization. By providing both positive and constructive feedback, you can help your team members understand their strengths and weaknesses, and identify areas where they can improve.

When providing feedback, it's important to be specific and objective. Focus on the individual's behavior or actions, rather than their personality or character. For example, instead of saying "you're not a good communicator," you could say "I noticed that in the meeting, you didn't provide enough context for the team to understand your point."

In addition to providing feedback, it's also important to ask for feedback from your team. This can help you understand how you're doing as a leader and identify areas where you can improve. Encourage your team members to be honest and direct in their feedback, and be open to their suggestions.

Finally, make sure to follow up on feedback and provide ongoing support and guidance as needed. This can help your team members continue to learn and grow, and can help them feel valued and supported in their roles.

Empowering employees to take risks and try new things is essential for fostering a culture of experimentation and innovation. Here are some tips for encouraging your team to take risks and try new things:

> **Set clear expectations:** Make sure your team understands what is expected of them and what the boundaries are for experimentation. Be clear about what risks are acceptable and which ones are not.

> **Provide resources and support:** Ensure your team has the necessary resources and support to experiment and take risks. This can include providing training, mentorship,

and access to tools and technology.

> **Encourage collaboration:** Encourage your team to collaborate and share their ideas with each other. This can help to spark new ideas and approaches and can create a sense of camaraderie and support.

> **Recognize and reward innovation:** Recognize and reward team members who take risks and try new things, even if their efforts are not always successful. This can encourage others to do the same and can help to create a culture of experimentation.

> **Foster a safe environment:** Create an environment where team members feel safe to take risks and try new things without fear of punishment or failure. Encourage open communication and honest feedback, and celebrate both successes and failures.

> **Trust your team:** Trust your team to make decisions and take risks. Provide guidance and support when needed, but also give them the autonomy to experiment and try new things.

Continuous innovation is critical for businesses to stay ahead of the competition. In today's rapidly changing business landscape, it's no longer enough to rely on past successes or keep doing things the same way. Customers are constantly seeking new and innovative products and services, and businesses that fail to keep up risk falling behind.

Continuous innovation involves constantly looking for ways to improve your products, services, and processes. It requires a willingness to take risks, experiment with new ideas, and learn from your successes and failures. By continuously innovating, businesses can stay ahead of the competition, attract new customers, and retain existing ones.

One of the key benefits of continuous innovation is that it helps businesses stay relevant. As customer needs and preferences change, businesses must adapt to meet those needs. By innovating and introducing new products and services, businesses can remain relevant and appeal to a wider audience.

Continuous innovation can also lead to increased efficiency and cost savings. By continuously improving processes, businesses can streamline operations, reduce waste, and increase productivity. This can result in cost savings that can be reinvested into the business or passed on to customers in the form of lower prices.

Another benefit of continuous innovation is that it can help businesses stay ahead of potential disruptors. Disruptive technologies or new market entrants can quickly shake up an industry, and businesses that are slow to adapt risk losing market share. By continuously innovating and staying ahead of the curve, businesses can better position themselves to fend off potential disruptors.

In summary, continuous innovation is critical for businesses to stay ahead of the competition in today's rapidly changing business landscape. By constantly looking for ways to improve and innovate, businesses can stay relevant, attract new customers, increase efficiency, and stay ahead of potential disruptors.

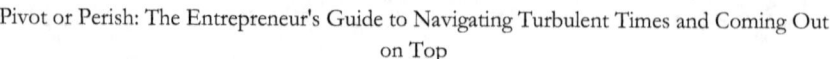

Chapter 8: Putting it All Together

A pivot roadmap is a plan that outlines the steps your business needs to take in order to pivot its strategy, operations, or product offerings in response to changing market conditions, customer needs, or other factors. Here are some steps you can follow to create a pivot roadmap for your business:

> **Assess the current state of your business:** Take a close look at your current strategy, operations, and product offerings, and evaluate how well they are performing in the current market. Identify any areas where your business is struggling or facing challenges.

> **Identify potential pivot opportunities:** Look for opportunities to pivot your strategy, operations, or product offerings in response to the challenges you identified. This might involve changing your target market, shifting your business model, or introducing new products or services.

> **Evaluate the potential impact of each pivot opportunity:** Consider the potential benefits and risks of each pivot opportunity, and evaluate how each one would impact your business in terms of revenue, profitability, and market share.

> **Develop a pivot roadmap:** Based on your assessment and evaluation, develop a plan that outlines the steps you need to take in order to pivot your business. This might include changes to your product offerings, marketing strategy, or organizational structure.

> **Implement the pivot roadmap:** Put your plan into action, and monitor its progress closely. Be prepared to adjust your strategy as needed based on market feedback and other factors.

> **Measure the success of your pivot:** Once you have implemented your pivot roadmap, evaluate its success in

terms of revenue growth, customer acquisition, and other key performance indicators. Use this information to further refine your strategy and continue to pivot as needed in response to changing market conditions.

Measuring success is critical for any business, particularly when implementing a pivot roadmap. To ensure that your pivot is working as intended, you need to track its progress and measure its success. Here are some tips for measuring success and adjusting course as needed:

➢ **Define your key performance indicators (KPIs):** Identify the metrics that will allow you to evaluate the success of your pivot roadmap. These metrics should be specific, measurable, and tied to your overall business goals.

➢ **Track and analyze data:** Collect data on your KPIs and use this data to track your progress. Analyze this data regularly to identify trends and make data-driven decisions about whether to stay the course or adjust your approach.

➢ **Adjust course as needed:** If your pivot isn't working as intended, don't be afraid to adjust your approach. Use the data you've collected to identify where things went wrong and what changes you can make to get back on track.

➢ **Celebrate successes:** Celebrate the successes you achieve along the way. Recognize and reward the hard work of your team members, and use these successes as motivation to keep moving forward.

➢ **Communicate with stakeholders:** Keep your stakeholders informed about your progress and any changes to your approach. This includes your team members, customers, investors, and other partners.

Continuous learning and improvement are critical for personal and professional growth, and for the success of any business. Here are some reasons why:

> **Stay Relevant:** As technology and market conditions change rapidly, it's essential to keep up with new developments to remain relevant. Continuous learning ensures that you and your team have the necessary skills and knowledge to adapt to these changes and stay competitive.

> **Improve Efficiency:** Continuous improvement helps identify and eliminate inefficiencies in processes, leading to cost savings and improved productivity. This can help your business operate more efficiently, increase profitability, and provide better value to customers.

> **Enhance Quality:** By continually learning and improving, businesses can deliver higher quality products and services to customers. This leads to better customer satisfaction, loyalty, and a strong reputation.

> **Foster Innovation:** Continuous learning and improvement can inspire creative thinking and spark innovation. This can lead to new products, services, and business models that set you apart from your competitors.

> **Employee Development:** Continuous learning and improvement opportunities can help employees feel valued and motivated, leading to increased job satisfaction and retention.

ABOUT THE AUTHOR

Thank you for reading book.

www.ingramcontent.com/pod-product-compliance
Lightning Source LLC
Chambersburg PA
CBHW070919220526
45467CB00004B/1480